The Ultimate Guide To Overcoming Shopping Addiction

The Most Effective, Permanent Solution To Finally Control Compulsive Shopping and Buying Disorder

John K.

Table of Contents

Introduction

Chapter 1 – Shopping Spree or Shopping Addiction?

Chapter 2 – Getting to the Root of the Problem

Chapter 3 – Recovering

Chapter 4 – Avoiding Relapse

Chapter 5 – Outlook for the Future

Conclusion

Check Out My Other Books

Introduction

I want to thank you and congratulate you for purchasing the book, *"The Ultimate Guide To Overcome Shopping Addiction: The Most Effective, Permanent Solution To Finally Control Compulsive Shopping and Buying Disorder".*

This book contains proven steps and strategies on how to overcome your shopping disorder, gain more self-confidence and get your life back in control.

Compulsive shopping disorder can wreck people's lives not just financially but also personally because it prevents the achievement of a normal and fulfilling human life. This book will teach you how to solve the problem by uprooting the main reason for your compulsion and by helping you build a better and stronger personality which can withstand future tendencies towards this disorder.

Thanks again for purchasing this book, I hope you enjoy it!

© **Copyright 2014 by John K. - All rights reserved.**

This document is geared towards providing exact and reliable information in regards to the topic and issue covered. The publication is sold with the idea that the publisher is not required to render accounting, officially permitted, or otherwise, qualified services. If advice is necessary, legal or professional, a practiced individual in the profession should be ordered.

- From a Declaration of Principles which was accepted and approved equally by a Committee of the American Bar Association and a Committee of Publishers and Associations.

In no way is it legal to reproduce, duplicate, or transmit any part of this document in either electronic means or in printed format. Recording of this publication is strictly prohibited and any storage of this document is not allowed unless with written permission from the publisher. All rights reserved.

The information provided herein is stated to be truthful and consistent, in that any liability, in terms of inattention or otherwise, by any usage or abuse of any policies, processes, or directions contained within is the solitary and utter responsibility of the recipient reader. Under no circumstances will any legal responsibility or blame be held against the publisher for any reparation, damages, or monetary loss due to the information herein, either directly or indirectly.

Respective authors own all copyrights not held by the publisher.

The information herein is offered for informational purposes solely, and is universal as so. The presentation of the information is without contract or any type of guarantee assurance.

The trademarks that are used are without any consent, and the publication of the trademark is without permission or backing by the trademark owner. All trademarks and brands within this book are for clarifying purposes only and are the owned by the owners themselves, not affiliated with this document.

Chapter 1 – Shopping Spree or Shopping Addiction?

It can be very difficult to determine whether you have a shopping addiction or simply love to shop because the modern lifestyle encourages people to constantly buy new stuff. Of course, it is also possible to criticize this tendency to shop constantly, but what makes constant shopping different from an addiction is the person who likes to shop does not feel *compelled* to shop in order to fill a need inside herself or to solve a problem which she may or may not understand. That is, she enjoys shopping and likes to have new stuff particularly if the designers or stores have released their new fashions, but if she is not able to shop for whatever reason, e.g. work responsibilities, financial limits, etc. then she is still able to function normally precisely because there is no need or problem the shopping is supposed to solve.

For example, let us say someone needs to pay her bills and will not have enough left to buy new shoes. Since she does not feel that she *needs* those shoes, she can forgo them to pay the bills. She may still *want* those shoes and plan to buy those shoes *after* she pays her bills or *after* she ensures that her financial responsibilities are met, but this is not the same as the *need* which the compulsive shopper feels.

In contrast, a person with a shopping disorder will dismiss her bills and go ahead and buy those shoes because she *needs* them. This does not mean that she is not worried about her bills, but since she feels *compelled* to buy new shoes, she swallows her worries and spends her money on the shoes.

At this point, it is important to distinguish between 'need' and 'want.' ==You *need* something when your life cannot proceed *normally* without it.== Thus, for your life to continue as it *normally* does, you need food, water, decent clothes, a vehicle or means of transportation, a decent house, etc. You *want* something when life can proceed normally without it. You *need* a car to take you to work, but you may *want* a better model. The desire for a better model is based on a *want*, e.g. you want to show off your economic status, you want to have a more comfortable ride, you want the extras provided by the better car model, etc.

Going back to our examples above, the person without a shopping addiction may feel bad about not being able to buy new shoes, but she can still function normally without them. She can still concentrate at work, still has sufficient self-esteem, and can reason with herself that she can buy the shoes at a later date. The person with a shopping addiction will not be able to function normally until she buys the shoes. She will not be able to concentrate at work, will have inadequate self-esteem and cannot accept any rational argument for not buying the shoes she does not actually need.

This need is what makes those with a shopping addiction feel compelled to buy new things. This is also why it is difficult to reach those with a true addiction through rational argument. Appeals to reason will not work on someone who thinks of shopping as a need. This would be like giving a rational argument to a hungry person on why he must not eat.

With the concept of 'need' in mind, we will then be able to distinguish between true addiction and an irrational tendency to go on shopping sprees. As we have mentioned, the modern lifestyle encourages people to constantly buy new things. Some people might be encouraged to buy because of their constant exposure to advertisements, but most of the time they only have an irrational want. Once they realize that they ought to curb their shopping because they already have financial problems or their closet if almost bursting, then they will be able to stop albeit reluctantly.

Sometimes these people are considered to have a shopping addiction albeit a very mild one. If this describes you, then you can also benefit from the tips suggested in this book. You are fortunate because you do not have a major root problem which serious shopping addicts suffer from. You can skip reading chapter 2 if you wish.

Meanwhile, the person with a serious shopping addiction has a *need* to shop because it fills something missing in their lives or makes them believe that it solves a problem. The problem can be clear or vague, and the sufferer may or may not be aware of it. For example, the sufferer may know that she compulsively shops to cure her loneliness or to fill in her lack of self-esteem. If so, then she can know that her problem can only be solved by focusing on the main reason for her addiction. Unfortunately, some sufferers may not know why they feel compelled to shop, or the reason may be too painful that they refuse to acknowledge it.

In this book, we will consider true shopping addicts to be those who feel compelled to shop because of a need which, if not fulfilled, disrupts the normal flow of their lives. Those who only feel an irrational want for new things are technically not addicted but they can still benefit from this book because it teaches them how to discipline their spending. There are also some people who are in between serious addiction and mere irrational lack of discipline.

You will know who you are depending on whether you consider shopping a need or want, and how much shopping disrupts your life.

Chapter 2 – Getting to the Root of the Problem

All addictions are either caused by or encouraged by a problem/s. Addictions are the excessive doing of activities or consumption of things which are valued for the pleasant feelings they contribute. For example, eating, shopping and drinking all give us pleasant feelings in addition to the other advantages they may give. Some people may be addicted to harmful activities like hurting themselves or being hurt by others, but it may be argued that they get some kind of pleasant feeling from these activities.

The pleasant feelings are good, but they cannot be considered the only good in a human being's life. A person still has to function or live normally, i.e. do his job, perform his social roles, etc. Anyone who does not function normally will be considered problematic. Some people will be more problematic than others if their addictions start to affect other people's lives.

This is not to say, of course, that those who do not affect others should be left on their own or are given an excuse to continue with their addictions. Many wealthy sufferers of shopping addiction say that if they can afford to shop anyway, then there is no problem. However, as we have mentioned in the previous chapter, the problem is not really financial though it can include that if the person is not financially well-off. The problem of shopping addiction is, like all addictions, the prevention of the sufferer to live a normal and fulfilling life.

No addiction sufferer can truthfully admit that she is happy. The addiction fuels a vicious cycle: a problem is unsolved resulting in the need for the pleasant feelings brought by the addiction, but the addiction still does not solve the problem so it continues. In serious cases, it can even increase in intensity where the sufferer must get more of what she is addicted to.

If you want to get out of this cycle, or if you want to help a friend, you must get to the root of the problem. Here are some questions which may help in order to know why the shopping addiction started:

- Was there a traumatic event which prompted the addiction, e.g. the death of a loved one, divorce or end of a significant relationship, loss of a job or financial troubles, etc.?

- Do you feel self-conscious about your personal flaws, either in your appearance or performance? Do you think you lack self-esteem? Do you constantly compare yourself with others and believe that you are inferior?

- ==Do you feel that there is something lacking in your life?== (This can either be clear to you or just be a vague feeling.)

These questions are only a general starting point. Once the problem is made clearer, it may be necessary to ask further questions. For example, if a self-esteem problem is admitted to, it may be asked whether this is caused by some other problem like an abusive relationship or is simply the result of a perceived personal flaw.

It is important that these questions be answered truthfully or else there will be no progress. It may be difficult to answer these questions so here are some tips to help you:

- Choose a time when you will be able to focus on these questions and really think about them. If necessary, take some time off work.

- Depending on your personality, you may go through this process alone or with the help of a trusted friend. If you are helping a friend with shopping addiction, then you must ask her how she wishes to do this step. You must respect her decision. Sometimes, being too helpful may be detrimental. To ensure that she completes this step, ask her to write down her answers to the questions above. Tell her that she must arrive at a definite answer as to the reason for her addiction.

- It is not necessary to complete this step in only one try. If you feel unable to focus, then try again another time. However, do not use this excuse to get out of this step or else you will never solve your addiction. Remind yourself that you need and want to solve your addiction because it will allow you to live a better life.

- Some people might find group support to be helpful. Look up group therapy sessions where people with similar addictions come together to discuss their problems and encourage each other to heal.

- For serious cases, do not hesitate to ask the help of a psychiatrist.

Once the root of the problem is clarified, it can be solved. What needs to be done will depend on the problem. For example, if the shopping addiction is caused by an abusive relationship which in turn causes low self-esteem, then the abusive relationship must be cut and exercises which raise the self-esteem must be done. If the problem is the inability to deal with a traumatic event, then alternative means to heal may be pursued like spiritual activities and seeking emotional support from friends.

Chapter 3 - Recovering

While this book cannot discuss the specifics on how to solve particular problems which caused shopping addiction, it can suggest ways to help sufferers recover quicker. Since the addiction is shopping, it will help remove all or at least most of the chances to return to that activity until the addiction is completely gone.

An alcoholic must remove all alcoholic drinks from his home and avoid activities which include drinking. This is easy to do since alcoholic drinks are not necessary in everyday life, but everybody must shop in one way or another to obtain necessities. Even if the shopping addict is addicted to shoes and clothes and she has started to avoid these items, the addiction can suddenly become a compulsion to buy unnecessary amounts of food. How should a shopping addict cope?

The easiest way to go about this is to ask someone else to do the shopping. If this is not possible, then a companion might help ensure that no extra items are bought. A shopping list will ensure that you only get what you need and nothing more. In the beginning, it might be necessary to be strict in this rule in order to make sure that the compulsion to shop is nipped in the bud. Thus, if something is not in the list, it must *not* be bought even if it is on sale.

For example, while grocery shopping, you might be tempted to stock up on canned items because they are marked half price off, but while the root problem of your addiction is not yet solved, this might be an opportunity to rekindle your addiction and destroy the progress you've made. To help you cope, remind yourself that that is not the last sale you will ever encounter in your life. Once you are recovered and are sure that you no longer have a shopping addiction, you can take advantage of sales and know that you are buying the items *because you wish to save money and not because you wish to feed your compulsion.*

It might also help to organize your closet and pantry to see how much you already have, what you really need and what you can remove from your home. This will likely be a painful process since the shopping addict gets comfort from the items she has bought; but just as the alcoholic must tear himself away from alcohol in order to be cured, you must also submit to this process. If necessary, do this with a friend who can be firm with you and will not allow you to make rationalizations to keep certain items.

Under no circumstances must unnecessary items be kept just in case they might be needed in the future. However, it is important to be reasonable here. If you need a winter coat, then you must keep the winter coat for when that season arrives. Perhaps you need 2 or 3 to match your various fashion looks, but there is probably no need to keep 2 or 3 identical styles just in case one gets accidentally ripped and need to be replaced.

If this common rationalization keeps popping up, the best way to destroy it is the reminder that it is still possible to buy necessary items in the future. Stores will not close and people will always have access to their needs. If your winter coat gets ripped or worn out, then you can replace it with a new one. In fact, it makes more sense to buy new things when they are needed rather than keep old things 'just in case.' It is difficult to know when a reserve coat might be needed, and by the time it is needed, the style might become outdated or it might already have signs of age like stains or moth holes. In addition, such items can take up too much space and might even cause hygiene problems. Insects like cockroaches might use these items for their home and they can gather dust and dirt.

Similar arguments can be given depending on the excess items you have. If you became addicted to make-up or food and have piles of unused items, then it may be pointed out that

==you cannot save these items 'just in case' because they have an expiration date.==

Depending on your financial situation, you may resell the items you don't need or donate them to charity.

To keep your mind away from shopping, it will help to start a hobby but try to pick one that is far removed from shopping. Obviously, it will not help you to start a hobby which requires you to buy new equipment. For example, you might think of knitting as a hobby then buy boxes of knitting needles and yarn plus various books on knitting. You might find yourself knitting more just so you can buy more yarn. If you must buy some items to start your hobby, ask someone else to do so.

What you do will depend on your interests and disposition. Some people like quiet activities while some need to get out and work. Whatever you do, make sure that you do not make rationalizations to shop. If you are more excited about shopping for things you need for your hobby than actually doing the hobby, then you are only fooling yourself.

A good option for a hobby which does not require any shopping is to volunteer for charity. In doing this, you might become more sensitive to the needs of others and stop wasting money on things you don't need. Another good option is to enjoy the company of your family and friends as long as you do not spend your time shopping. Regularly bonding with good people who love you will also help improve your self-esteem and give you emotional support while you are still solving the root problem of your shopping addiction.

You should stay away from stores, online shopping sites and TV shopping channels. If necessary, cancel your credit card and bring only a reasonable amount of cash for your daily needs, or else use a debit card which informs you of how much money you still have. If you work outside your home, perhaps you can bring your own lunch to avoid the need to buy food. Ask other people to not make you meet them in stores or shopping malls.

These may seem like drastic measures, but what you need to do will always depend on how serious your addiction is. If you feel that you can go to a shopping mall and will not have the compulsion to shop as long as you don't have a credit card, then by all means do so. However, if you find yourself using your gas money to buy something and consequently have to take the bus home, or worse, have to walk, then your addiction is more serious and you must take more drastic measures to avoid the temptation to shop.

If you are not sure how drastic your measures should be, consult a friend or psychiatrist who can remain objective about your situation.

Chapter 4 – Avoiding Relapse

The most dangerous time when solving an addiction is the period after the root problem is solved. This is the time when relapses can occur and the addiction starts all over again. Fortunately, this does not mean all hope is lost. Since the root problem is already determined, it is only necessary to remain vigilant in ensuring that it does not come back.

You can avoid relapse by following the tips listed in the previous chapter. Again, what you need to do will depend on your particular situation. You might be able to meet people in shopping malls but still feel that you must leave your credit card behind. You might feel strong enough to take a credit card with you but have to hide it in a separate wallet with a note that says 'only for emergencies' in big letters.

If ever you break down and start compulsive shopping again, resist the urge to judge yourself too harshly. You must try to remember what triggered you to start shopping and try to solve that problem. This might be frustrating at first, but the point is you are trying to become a better person. If you fail, then pick yourself up and go through the necessary processes again.

Whatever you do, do not compare yourself with other people who have made a quicker recovery. Your situation is unique and must be solved in a unique way. What is more important is you wish to be healed and are on your way to recovery.

Chapter 5 – Outlook for the Future

Whether your shopping addiction will return or not depends on various factors. These factors may include how serious your addiction was, the root problem of the addiction and whether this was completely solved or not.

Regardless, to help you become a stronger person who can better resist the urge to shop compulsively again, here are some tips:

1. Seek financial advice and track your spending. The more responsible you are about money, the less likely will you return to your previous addiction. If you are responsible about money, you will understand the need to save for your retirement and to invest wisely. Since your money goes to your savings or investments, you will be less tempted to spend it on random and temporary things.

2. By all means necessary, avoid debt especially credit card debt. This is actually an application of the first tip.

Credit cards allow you to spend even if you technically have no money. Since you don't see the amounts pile up until the bill arrives, it gives you an impression of unlimited spending power. On the other hand, if you pay with cash or a debit card, you will know how much money you still have. This will make you a more responsible spender.

3. Buy only what you need and never stock up on any item by giving the rationalization 'just in case.' We have already discussed the reason for this in chapter 3.

4. Do not allow yourself to be tempted by sales. While this is a great way to save money, it can also make you buy more than what you need. The best way to treat sales is to disregard them completely and simply buy what you need when you need them. For example, if you only need 1 shirt, then buy only 1 shirt even if the price is 20% off. While this might seem as if you have not taken advantage of the sale, remind yourself that you have already saved 20% of the regular price by buying that 1 shirt. If you buy 2 shirts rather than just 1, then you have actually *not* saved at all

because you bought something you don't need.

5. Sometimes stores can be tricky and give you a discount only if you buy 2 shirts, but there will be no discount if you buy 1. What should you do if you only need 1 shirt? It is important to understand that sales exist to help you save money. Unfortunately, the stores take advantage of the modern consumerist culture to make sales entice people to buy more. If you need to buy 1 shirt anyway, then you would buy that item regardless whether there is a sale or not. Thus, the best way to avoid the temptation to buy more is always to disregard sales completely and simply buy what you need.

6. An alternative to the solution in #5 is to buy 2 shirts to get the discount, but to not buy any more shirts until you need a new one. Since you have 2 new shirts, it must take you a longer time to need to shop for shirts again.

7. Give yourself an occasional treat. While it is important to buy only what you need, there will be times when you find something you don't need but would like to have or would like to try out. For

example, you find an interesting, one-of-a-kind dress or a new brand of food item. Consider this your shopping treat similar to the piece of dessert dieters use to treat themselves so they won't feel deprived.

8. However, you must always treat yourself responsibly. A treat must remain a treat. It is a pleasing extravagance to make your life more interesting, but it is not a need. How often you give yourself a shopping treat will depend on what that treat is and how much it costs. If it is a new food item you wish to taste and costs only a few bucks, then you can probably give yourself this treat on a weekly basis. If it is a piece of expensive clothing or jewelry, then it will be unreasonable to treat yourself every month. To help you remain disciplined, you should take note of your treats when you track your spending.

9. Be wary of small or cheap items. Just as sales can make you forget your shopping discipline, buying small items can make you forget how much you are spending. Pennies can add up to a few dollars and a few dollars can add up to a few hundreds, and so on.

Conclusion

Thank you again for purchasing this book!

I hope this book was able to help you to overcome your shopping addiction.

The next step is to try the tips listed here to know what works for you.

Finally, if you enjoyed this book, then I'd like to ask you for a favor, would you be kind enough to leave a review for this book on Amazon? It'd be greatly appreciated!

Thank you and good luck!

Check Out My Other Books

Below you'll find some of my other popular books that are popular on Amazon and Kindle as well. Simply click on the links below to check them out. Alternatively, you can visit my author page on Amazon to see other work done by me. If the links do not work, for whatever reason, you can simply search for these titles on the Amazon website to find them.

1) The Ultimate Guide To Overcome Anger - How To Manage Your Anger Before It Controls You

go to: http://amzn.to/1Pzm3Yy

2) The Ultimate Guide To Become An Alpha Male - How To Attract Women, Win In Life And Be Confident

go to: http://amzn.to/20G8bB0

3) **The Ultimate Guide To Overcome Porn Addiction For Life - The Most Effective, Permanent Solution To Finally Stop Porn Addiction**

go to: http://amzn.to/1NZ2tmN

4) **The Drug Addiction Cure - The Most Effective, Permanent Solution to Finally Overcome Drug Addiction for Life**

go to: http://amzn.to/1kkb9uc

5) How to Stop Snoring for Life - The Most Effective Cures and Remedies for Snoring

go to: http://amzn.to/1NE9uLn

Made in United States
North Haven, CT
18 April 2024

51470068R00021